The Story of Sister Clara Mohammed & The First Islamic School in North America

Safiyyah Shahid

edited by Qur'an Shakir
illustrations by Allen London
and
Qur'an Shakir with support from
Microsoft Bing Image Creator

BUBI (Building Us Beyond Imagination) Publishing
All rights reserved
2025

ISBN: 978-1-966132-02-8

sharingourlegacy@gmail.com

Dedication

To my children, grandchildren, great-grandchildren,
and to every little Muslim child who needs to know
you are a part of something sacred, brave,
and beautifully built.

This book is for you.
It is a seed from a tree planted long ago
—watered with prayer, lifted by vision, and
tended by hands that believed in the
promise of YOUR future.

I offer these pages as a glimpse
into how our community, guided by the light of
Imam W. D. Mohammed, dared to educate
its own in a time when doing so
felt impossible. We rose anyway.

Let this be a reminder that our stories matter.
And if you don't write it down, it didn't happen.

May you read, may you grow,
and may you one day write what happens next.

With love and sincerity,
Safiyyah Shahid

*If you
don't
write it down,
it did not
happen!*

Have you heard of Sister Clara Mohammed, the brave and determined woman who changed her whole community—and even the world—by believing in herself and helping others?

Sister Clara Mohammed was born November 2, 1899 at the turn of the 20th century, in Cordele, Georgia. Her name at birth was Clara Evans. Her parents were Quartus Evans and Mary Lou (Thomas) Evans.

In 1917, she married Elijah Poole who was the son of sharecroppers. He was from a Georgia town called Sandersville. Their 55-year marriage produced six sons and two daughters.

In 1923, after the birth of two children --Ethel and Emmanuel, Clara and Elijah and their small family moved to Detroit, Michigan, a journey North that more than 6 million African Americans undertook for better economic opportunities and better living conditions. This movement was called The Great Migration

Sister Clara Mohammed, called Sister Clara by those who knew and loved her, was a wonderful wife and mother. She helped her husband, now known as Elijah Mohammed, in his mission of uplifting African American people to high morals and respect and dignity for themselves.

Learn and grow, build and lead—
"Do for self" was her creed!

She also set up classes for the women called Muslim Girls Training and General Civilization Class (MGT, GCC). She taught them how to sew, cook, clean, take care of their children, their husbands, and their homes.

This work that she and her husband were doing was like a movement to empower Black people. They called their community the Nation of Islam. Her husband became the leader and was now called the Honorable Elijah Mohammed.

Learn and grow, build and lead—
"Do for self" was their creed!

Sister Clara was also concerned about the kind of education her children were receiving in the public school system. Day after day, her children came home from school sad and crying, "They are talking about us saying people of color are from monkeys, that we were swinging on trees in Africa, and that our people are not civilized."

Because these things were not true, this made Sister Clara concerned about the kind of education her children and others were receiving in the public schools. She wanted them to know and feel proud about their African heritage, their brilliance as descendants of great builders, scientists, agriculturalists, theologians, and leaders. She decided to start teaching her own children in the family living room at her home. Her decision, however, did not go unnoticed with the public school officials.

Officials in the public school system and the police in Detroit, Michigan told Sister Clara that teaching her children at home was against the law. They came to her home and told her to stop. They tried to take her children away from her.

Sister Clara, a strong and courageous woman, told the police, "I'll be deader than this doorknob before I allow you to put my children in your public schools."

Learn and grow, build and lead—
"Do for self" was her creed!

Brave and determined like Sister Clara, many Nation of Islam families started teaching children at home. "We're doing for ourselves!" they said proudly.

From this humble beginning, the Clara Mohammed School system began. Sis. Clara established one of the earliest religious homeschooling programs in the United States. She named this primary and secondary school the University of Islam to inspire students with the idea of a great education.

From 1935 to 1946, there were many challenges. Because some people disagreed with the way her husband, The Honorable Elijah Mohammed, was leading the community, they tried to take over. It was a difficult and dangerous time, and Sister Clara knew she had to stay strong to protect her family and the people who looked up to them.

Then, something even more challenging happened during this time. The Honorable Elijah Mohammed was sent to prison because he didn't join the military during a big event called World War II. He questioned, "Aren't I too old to serve in the military? I don't understand why you are imprisoning me."

Sister Clara was left to take care of their children and the entire community. It was a lot of responsibility, but Sister Clara was not afraid.

She reminded everyone that they had to stick together and work hard, no matter what challenges they faced. She encouraged them to keep learning, keep praying, and keep believing in themselves. Even though times were tough, Sister Clara showed incredible strength and courage.

She made sure the school continued to grow as similar schools were established in many North American cities. The schools were teaching children that they could be leaders too.

The community respected Sister Clara for her wisdom and bravery. She inspired everyone to stand tall and remember that together, they could overcome any obstacle.

After the passing of the Honorable Elijah Mohammed, Wallace, the son of Elijah and Clara, became the new leader of the Muslim community in 1975. In 1977, Wallace, now called Imam W.D. Mohammed, renamed the schools The Sister Clara Mohammed Schools.

He did this in honor of the dedication and sacrifices his mother had made in holding the community together while the Honorable Elijah Mohammed, her husband, his father, was away from the community.

Decades later, the wonderful school in Atlanta, Georgia and other cities in North America exist because Sister Clara Mohammed believed in Muslims educating their own children in Muslim schools. Atlanta opened its school in 1965. There are even schools in Bermuda and Belize outside of the United States.

Many of these schools were accredited by national and regional accrediting bodies, surpassing rigorous standards of quality and sustainability. Graduates of these schools have received scholarships and advanced degrees throughout the country.

Sister Clara Mohammed lived to be 72 years old. The whole community was saddened by her passing in August 1972. But, there was a commitment to continue her legacy of educating and ensuring that all children, especially children of color, could learn about their heritage, learn to celebrate their brilliance, and could learn and grow, build and lead following the Clara Mohammed 'Do For Self' creed.

May the legacy of Sister Clara Mohammed live on in the thousands that have been educated through the school system that she envisioned in 1933. Ameen.

Learn and grow,
Build and lead—
"Do for self"
was her creed!

Appendix

Cultural and Social Topics
- The importance of education in the African American struggle for empowerment, 17
- The role of women leaders in shaping communities and movements, 17, 18, 19. 20
- What "Do for Self" means, 20
- Ways "Do for Self" was practiced in Sister Clara's time, 15. 20

Historical Context
- Birth of Sister Clara, 2
- Birth name of Sister Clara, 2
- Birth name of Sister Clara's husband, 4
- Birthplace of Sister Clara, 2
- Birthplace of Sister Clara's husband, 3
- Children of Sis. Clara and Elijah Mohammed, 4, 18, 19, 24
- The Great Migration and its impact on African American communities, 4
- World War II and its effects on Black Americans, 15

Religious and Philosophical Themes
- Explanation of the principles of the Nation of Islam during the 1930s-1940s, 10, 11, 13, 17. 27
- The role of faith and perseverance in overcoming adversity, 17, 18. 19
- How Sister Clara Mohammed's actions aligned with broader social justice movements, 15, 18, 24, 27

Definitions and Explanations
  - Conscientious Objector, 15
  - Great Migration, 4
  - Colonization,
  - Empowerment, 17
  - Homeschooling, 15, 17
  - Community building, 16

Words to Know

- Look at the "Words to Know".
- Find where each word shows up in Sister Clara's story.
- How does this word help you to understand what Sister Clara Mohammed went through or believed in?

believe
brave
brilliance
century
civilize
creed
community
descendants
determined
dignity
empower
envision
expel
heritage
honorable
humble
incredible
legacy
mission
morals
obstacles
overcome
respect
sacrifice
sharecroppers
unity

Think and Reflect

- How do you think Sister Clara Mohammed showed bravery and determination in her life?

- Why do you think education was so important to Sister Clara Mohammed and her community?

- What does "Do for Self" mean to you, and how can you practice it in your own life?

- Why is it important to stand up for what you believe, even when it's hard?

- How can you help your community grow and become stronger, like Sister Clara did?

- If you couldn't go to school and had to learn at home during a hard time, what would you want to learn? Who would teach you?

- Look at words "segregation", "education", or "leader", and think about:
    - What did this word mean in Sister Clara's time?
    - What does it mean for us today?

Activities to Learn More

- **World War II**
    - Research when and why our country joined other countries in World War II (WWII). Find out how WWII affected everyday people in the United States. What is the age that most men were drafted or required to fight in the war? Find out what jobs people took, how families supported soldiers, and how life changed during wartime. Write a short journal entry as if you lived during that time.
- **Conscientious Objector**
    - Find out what a conscientious objector is and why some people choose not to fight in wars. Write down three reasons someone might become a conscientious objector and how they might serve their country in other ways.
- **The Great Migration**
    - Look up why many African Americans moved from the South to northern cities like Detroit. What are the years that are called the years of the Great Migration? Create a map showing the journey from one southern city to a northern one and write a sentence about why families made the move.
- **The Great Depression**
    - Explore how people helped one another: shared food, made clothes by hand, and worked together in their communities during the 1930s when the stock market crashed in 1929. This helps young readers see how Sister Clara's choice to homeschool and "Do for Self" fit into a larger spirit of survival and strength.
    - Learn how Black communities were often hit even harder by the Great Depression and faced racism in jobs, schools, and housing which shows how building our own schools and teaching our own children was a powerful answer to injustice.
- **The State of the Black Community**
    - Find pictures or stories of African American communities during the 1930s and 1940s. Make a list of the challenges they faced and the ways they worked together to create better lives for themselves.
    - Find pictures or stories of African American communities today (at least the last 10 years). Make a list of the challenges they face and the ways they work together to create better lives for themselves.
    - Write an article or a description to compare and contrast the state of the Black Community now and in the past.
- **Colonization in the U.S.A. and Around the Globe**
    - Research the meaning of colonization. Which countries have been most apt to colonize other countries? Find one example of colonization, either in the U.S. or another country. Draw a picture or write a paragraph showing how colonization changed the lives of the people who lived there.

Sister Clara Mohammed Schools

(aka University of Islam)

in North America

1933 - 1979

This is an estimated list from various files and primary sources. It was difficult to find a complete listing.

Arizona
- Phoenix

Arkansas
- Little Rock

California
- Los Angeles
- Oakland
- San Francisco
- Stockton

Colorado
- Denver

Connecticut
- Hamden

Delaware
- Wilmington

District of Columbia
- Washington

Florida
- Miami

Georgia
- Atlanta
- Savannah

Illinois
- Chicago

Indiana
- Indianapolis

Kentucky
- Louisville

Louisiana
- Baton Rouge
- New Orleans

Maryland
- Baltimore

Massachusetts
- Boston

Michigan
- Detroit

Mississippi
- New Medinah

Missouri
- Kansas City
- St. Louis

New Jersey
- Camden
- Newark

New York
- Bronx
- Brooklyn
- New York
- Corona Queens

Nevada

North Carolina
- Charlotte
- Raleigh

Ohio
- Cleveland
- Cincinnati

Oklahoma
- Oklahoma City

Pennsylvania
- Philadelphia
- Pittsburgh

South Carolina
- Columbia
- Greenville

Tennessee
- Nashville

Texas
- Austin
- Dallas
- Houston

Virginia
- Green Bay
- Petersburg
- Richmond

Washington D.C.

Wisconsin
- Milwaukee

Outside the USA
- Bermuda, Hamilton
- Belize, MX

Sister Clara Mohammed Schools
in North America
Presently open

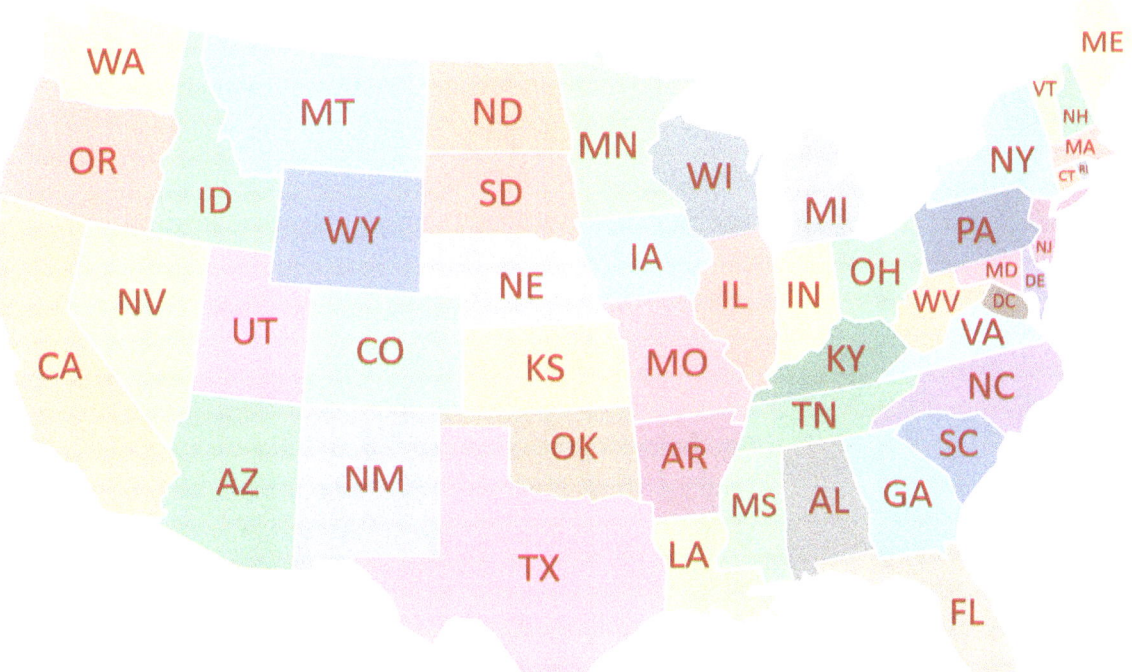

Arkansas
- Little Rock

California
- Los Angeles

Florida
- Miami

Georgia
- Atlanta
- Decatur

Illinois
- Chicago

Indiana
- Indianapolis

Michigan
- Detroit

Missouri
- St. Louis

New Jersey
- Camden
- Newark

New York
- Brooklyn
- New York
- Corona Queens

North Carolina
- Charlotte
- Fayetteville
- Raleigh

Online / Virtual
- New Medina
- New African Ummah Online School

Pennsylvania
- Philadelphia

South Carolina
- Charleston
- Columbia

Virginia
- Richmond

Washington D.C.

Wisconsin
- Milwaukee

Outside the USA
- Bermuda, Hamilton
- Belize, MX

...

Visit www.cmsnetwork.org for a complete listing of current schools inspired by Sister Clara Mohammed, as well as which schools are full time, weekend, or online and to see the grade levels of the schools.

About the Author

Safiyyah Shahid

is a proud mother, teacher, and leader who loves helping young people grow into their best selves. She started teaching many years ago. From teaching Muslim Girls Training classes to leading Mohammed Schools as principal, she has spent decades uplifting her community through learning, leadership, and service.

She holds degrees from Spelman College and Troy University and was selected by Imam W.D. Mohammed to join an education delegation to Saudi Arabia. Named Muslim Woman of the Year and one of Georgia's 100 Most Influential Muslims, she continues to mentor, serve, and inspire.

She has traveled the world, won awards, and worked hard to make schools better for everyone.

Now, she's sharing her first children's book—with many more on the way!

Safiyyah Shahid believes learning never stops, and she hopes this story inspires you to be brave, kind, and ready to "Do for Self!"

About the Illustrator

Allen London, known as "The Comeback Man," was a gifted artist, storyteller, and servant of his community. Born in Atlanta, Georgia, in 1953, Allen began drawing before he could read and turned his talent into a lifelong mission to uplift others. He created art for world-renowned entertainers and later used his gift to share the beauty of Islam, the strength of resilience, and the power of faith. After surviving a near-fatal accident in 1996 and living with a traumatic brain injury, Allen devoted his life to inspiring others through his drawings and community work. Before he passed in July 2024, Allen completed the heartfelt illustrations for this book about Sister Clara Mohammed—an effort that reflects his deep love for his faith, his people, and the enduring legacy of Muslim pioneers. His art is a testament to his belief in the Wondrous Creator and the ability to rise, rebuild, and rejoice—no matter the challenge.

About the Editor

Qur'an Shakir aka Madame Q is a master educator, author, and visionary editor with over four decades of experience in teaching, leadership, and curriculum development. As an editor, she brings a deep understanding of storytelling as a tool for healing, empowerment, and transformation. Her passion lies in elevating voices that celebrate self-discovery, womanhood, Black excellence, and emotional wellness. Madame Q is the founder of B.U.B.I. Publishing (Building Us Beyond Imagination), where she curates and publishes works that honor the legacy of her ancestors while inspiring new generations to grow beyond limitations. Her thoughtful editing approach helps authors shape powerful, purpose-filled messages that uplift communities and speak directly to the heart.

Editorial Support

Allison Smith is a lifelong learner and master teacher of more than 20 years. She earned her Bachelor's and Master's degrees from Florida A&M University in English and English education, respectively. She creates in her happy space which she shares with her husband of 28 years and their 4 children.

Dr. Cassandra M. El-Amin, PhD, A former teacher at the Muhammad University of Islam #15 in Atlanta, Georgia, she is a beloved educator and seasoned college professor who has dedicated over 30 years to shaping minds on the university level. Her commitment to teaching, research, and service in the field of education and reading continues to leave a lasting impact on generations of learners.

Crystal Shahid, daughter of Safiyyah Shahid, is a proud member of the first graduating class of Atlanta's Warith Deen Mohammed High School (WDMH) in 1992. A dedicated alumna, Crystal remains deeply involved as an active member of the Mohammed Schools of Atlanta volunteer group. She enrolled her own children in Mohammed Schools and now continues to invest in Islamic education by supporting her grandson on his journey through Mohammed Schools of Atlanta, In-sha-Allah, for many years to come.

About B.U.B.I. (Building Us Beyond Imagination) Publishing

B.U.B.I. Publishing (Building Us Beyond Imagination Publishing) is a mission-driven publishing company founded by Qur'an Shakir, affectionately known as Madame Q, who says she name the publishing company B.U.B.I. as an acronym for Building Us Beyond Imagination, and as a tribute to her ancestors who were stolen from this island hundreds of years ago, and brought to the Americas as enslaved Africans.

B.U.B.I. Publishing is dedicated to uplifting the voices of children who write, teachers who write, and aspiring authors with a passion for storytelling that heals, inspires, and builds strong communities.

Our focus is on literature that celebrates creation and the Creator, encourages healing and self-love, and supports mental, emotional, and spiritual well-being. Through children's books, educational works, and empowering stories, we strive to nurture a healthier, stronger sense of family and community. At B.U.B.I. Publishing, we believe in the power of words to help us grow beyond imagination—into our best, most authentic selves.

"Thank you www.africanancestry.com for helping our family to discover that we are from the Bubi Tribe on the Bioko Island, an island near Equitorial Guinea, West Africa."

References

Abdus-Sabur, Beverly and Dr. Qadir   Education: Our Number 1 Priority: Vision to Reality October 20, 2019

Mohammed-Ali, Halimah, In Her Spirit: A Narrative Biography on the Life of Clara Muhammad | 2010

Muhammad, Dr. Ramona Zakiyyah (1945–2019), Mother of the Nation: Clara Evans Muhammad: Wife of Elijah Muhammad, Mother of Imam W. Deen Mohammed, Institute of Muslim American Studies | July 30, 2020

www.ingramcontent.com/pod-product-compliance
Lightning Source LLC
Chambersburg PA
CBHW061350010526
44107CB00011B/885